T0354984

THE
PANDEMIC

JONI ELSNER

authorHOUSE®

AuthorHouse™
1663 Liberty Drive
Bloomington, IN 47403
www.authorhouse.com
Phone: 833-262-8899

Published by AuthorHouse 08/31/2021

ISBN: 978-1-6655-3706-3 (sc)
ISBN: 978-1-6655-3708-7 (e)

Library of Congress Control Number: 2021917903

Print information available on the last page.

Any people depicted in stock imagery provided by Getty Images are models,
and such images are being used for illustrative purposes only.
Certain stock imagery © Getty Images.

This book is printed on acid-free paper.

Because of the dynamic nature of the Internet, any web addresses or links contained in
this book may have changed since publication and may no longer be valid. The views
expressed in this work are solely those of the author and do not necessarily reflect the
views of the publisher, and the publisher hereby disclaims any responsibility for them.

Contents

Contents

Special Note

The content of this book is based on research and my own personal views. In no way will I ask you to adopt my views. I encourage independent thinking, research and drawing your own conclusion. I do use a little humor and a little sarcasm.

Dedication

This book is dedicated to the entire world for those that lived through the pandemic and lost loved ones. Never forget those that suffered mentally, financially, emotionally and had a hard time putting food on the table. For those that lost their jobs and for those that continued to work as essential workers. For the children that were not allowed to go to school, be in sports, and have birthday parties. We also need to remember those that were left in abusive situations with no place to go.

We need to give thanks to all of our first responders and anyone who put their life on the line for the safety of others.

While I was writing this book my sister-in-law Laura passed away and I would also like to dedicate this book to her.

To my dad, he always taught us to stand up for what we believe in and I miss him dearly. RIP dad.

God Bless You All.

Introduction

2020 was one of the most devastating years that any of us had to live through. It all started with a laboratory in Wuhan, China. A disease that was unleashed on the entire world.

On December 31, 2019 the World Health Organization (WHO) confirmed that dozens of people in Wuhan, China were being treated for pneumonia they believed the origin of the pneumonia came from a live animal market. Later it was determined it was not from the animal market but from a laboratory in Wuhan, China.

It was not until January 11, 2020 "Chinese state media reports the first death from novel coronavirus." [1]

"SEATTLE, Wash. — On January 21, 2020, the United States announced its first confirmed case of a disease caused by the novel coronavirus from Wuhan, China — what we now call COVID-19." [2] We did not know the first thing about this virus. We did not know how it was transmitted. What caused it or how to treat it. We did not even know the dangers or that it would target our elderly.

Dr. Li-Meng Yan a Chinese virologist "told Fox News in an exclusive interview that she believes the Chinese government knew about the novel coronavirus well before it claimed it did. She says her supervisors, renowned as some of the top experts in the field, also ignored research she was doing at the onset of the pandemic that she believes could have saved lives.)" [3] I remember watching this interview on television and my heart ached for this woman because I knew she was risking her life by telling the world the truth. She left her family behind and that could not have been easy. At the same time, I was very angry that China and the World Health Organization (WHO) tried to keep this from us. The United States paid a lot of money to belong to the World Health Organization and I believe this is why President Trump pulled us out of the WHO, and rightfully so. Our tax paying dollars were paying for this. Why should our tax dollars go to pay for things we don't believe in or pay for something that will destroy our own country?

On January 30, 2020 the Who Director "declared the 2019 CoV outbreak a Public Health Emergency of International Concern." [4]

January 31, 2020 President Trump signed an executive order blocking the entrance from those whom had been in China in the last 14 days and the order went into effect on February 2, 2020. [5]

This pandemic will go down history as the rest of the story unfolds, we are still finding out more each day. We have been scammed in my opinion. Do you honestly think that we needed the lock downs and mask mandates?

Why was it so important that we be censored for asking questions? I know a lot of doctors and scientist were censored for giving their expert opinions on treatment plans and mask mandates.

When does a conspiracy theory stop being a conspiracy theory? It stops when someone in a prominent position tells us that it is true. A prime example is that for years the government has denied that UFOs existed and some media outlets echoed the government. Now all of the sudden this year 2021 the government admits that UFOs exist and the media are reporting it.

How many other conspiracy theories are true?

The short version of the story is that the US was sending money to the Wuhan lab in the form of grants through another company. Why would anyone trust China? Fauci denied that he knew anything about the gain of function research that was going on in the lab. He just trusted China. They were working on making the SARs virus more deadly. I personally feel this was to be used as bio warfare.

There does need to be an investigation into Wuhan lab but I don't think Dr. Fauci should be a part of that investigation. It would be a conflict of interest. I don't really believe the Chinese will be forth coming. Do you see the hypocracy?

Chapter 1

The Coronavirus/COVID-19

As many of you already know, the coronavirus, later named COVID-19, came from a lab in Wuhan, China. It is crazy, but some called President Trump racist for calling it the China virus or flu. I certainly do not remember people getting out of sorts when the Spanish flu was called the Spanish flu no one called it racist.

"A Berkley research scientist names Xiao Qiang was monitoring China's statements about the virus and noticed that the World Health Organization (WHO) was echoing the same statements as China's messages."[1] Another doctor, "Dr. Li Wenliang was a thirty-four-year-old ophthalmologist at Wuhan Central Hospital in China's Hubei Province who was reprimanded by the Chinese government and later died of coronavirus after he warned others about the disease in late December."[2] This appears to be a sad twist in the story and a little suspicious to me. Later, I was watching the Tucker Carlson show, and he was interviewing a "Dr. Li-Meng Yan A top virologist that worked on the virus in Wuhan, she believes that the virus was manipulated and intentionally unleashed on the World."[3] You can watch the YouTube video at https://www.youtube.com/watch?v=PKMJiiCyhVc. Tucker Carlson interviewed her again at a later date, and she said the Chinese were trying to silence her by arresting her sixty-three-year-old mother.[4] You can see the video at https://video.foxnews.com/v/6198164324001#sp=show-clips. How deplorable that the Chinese would stoop so low as to arrest a sixty-three-year-old woman and mother just to silence her daughter for telling the truth. It makes them look guilty. It only confirms suspicions that they indeed unleashed this deadly virus upon the world. But why? Was it an accident? Was it to kill Americans? Was there another agenda? I do not think that we will ever get the truth from the Chinese government.

The hypocrisy is that our government, the good old United States, used our hard-earned taxpayer dollars to fund this lab.

> Dr. Anthony Fauci, a member of the coronavirus task force, had previously backed funding for a <u>controversial lab</u> in Wuhan, China, that has been studying the coronavirus in bats, reports said.
> Fauci's National Institute of Allergy and Infectious Diseases had shelled out a total of $7.4 million to the Wuhan Institute of Virology lab—which has become the focus of theories about the origin of COVID-19, <u>according to Newsweek</u>.[5]

We will have a whole chapter on Dr. Anthony Fauci because new information seems to be coming out in his emails.

Here is where the rhetoric begins. You have crazy Nancy Pelosi, speaker of the house, saying we should come to Chinatown and those precautions have been taken. I don't know what kind of precautions she was talking about because she was not wearing a mask; she was seen in a video hugging someone from the community and was surrounded by community members. You can watch the video at <u>https://youtu.be/CmllqkU6j2k</u>. By the way, I must say she was downplaying the situation. This occurred on February 24, 2020.[6] The hypocrisy is that later she accused our president of downplaying the virus and said he was not taking this seriously. What a hypocrite, Nancy. Why would she try to undermine the president of the United States? She was the one not taking the virus seriously. She was not wearing a mask or social distancing in Chinatown. This is the same woman that hopped on a plane to go get her hair done in a shop that was closed to the public. She was not wearing a mask once again.

When she got caught, she said she was set up. I wonder if that excuse works for criminals. Do you see the hypocrisy here? The shop was closed to the public; that means that the employees and shop owner could not make any money. They were closed to the public, so they should have been closed to Nancy Pelosi as well. There seems to be two sets of rules: one for the elite and another set for the rest of us.

"The next day, after the president declared a travel ban, you had Biden tweeting that the president had a "record of hysteria, xenophobia, and fear-mongering."[7] Then in March, Biden said when he said "xenophobic," he was referring to the president calling COVID-19 the Chinese virus. (No one ever commented on the Spanish flu that I remember. They never called it racist). Well, Mr. Biden, that is where the virus came from.

"During the 2009 N1H1 swine flu pandemic, the Obama administration with Joe Biden as VP at the time suddenly told states to shut down their testing, without providing much of an explanation. And, Biden's top advisor at the time has acknowledged that the Obama administration didn't do 'anything right' to combat that pandemic, before walking back those comments."[8] Do you see the hypocrisy? First Nancy and Joe criticized our president for moving too fast, then later, as it got closer to the reelection, they made the virus political. We will get into that in another chapter. Then Nancy and Joe criticized our president for not moving fast enough.

Diane Feinstein was caught at an airport not wearing a mask, but the airport workers were required to wear one. She is the senator that wanted a mask mandate for all airline employees and passengers. She said masks were important.[9] See what they do when they think no one is looking? See the hypocrisy? There is one set of rules for the elite and another set for the rest of us.

Dr. Fauci was seen at a game sitting next to two friends not wearing a mask. See the video: https://www.bing.com/videos/search?q=fauci+on+youtube+at+game+not+wearing+a+mask&docid=6080511731738347 18&mid=5F9FC474D1F509032BE35F9FC474D1F509032BE3&view =detail&FORM=VIRE.[10] At this point, a lot of people have lost faith in Dr. Fauci, and some see him as a fraud.

Then we have the great Chris Cuomo, and I am being sarcastic. Chris Cuomo has been caught many times not wearing a mask and even was told he could be fined for running around his apartment complex for not wearing a mask.[11] Tonight I saw him on the Tucker Carlson show, wanting a mask mandate and saying there should be sanctions because people could be killed. Gee, I guess that does not apply to him but applies to the rest of us. Do you see the hypocrisy?

Governor <u>Andrew Cuomo</u> of New York was not the only state leader to have directed nursing homes to admit patients who had been hospitalized for <u>COVID-19</u>. Governors from Michigan, California, New Jersey, and Pennsylvania, all Democrats, enacted similar policies last year as fears grew, those hospitals would be overwhelmed with new patients and too few health care providers.[12] I do not think that we will ever really truly know how many lives were lost because of the choices these governors made or because of all the shady deceptions that took place.

Another issue presented was the treatment of COVID-19. The president believed that hydroxychloroquine would work against the virus, and Dr. Fauci disagreed. "White House coronavirus advisor Dr. Anthony Fauci said that all the 'valid' scientific data shows hydroxychloroquine isn't effective in treating Covid-19."[13] Hydroxychloroquine has been around for a long time. It was a drug that was used to treat malaria, but like most drugs, it can be used for other things. I was personally on hydroxychloroquine for psoriatic arthritis. Doctors around the world have used hydroxychloroquine successfully in treating patients along with antibiotics and zinc. Some of America's frontline doctors believed that hydroxychloroquine does work. See the video: <u>https://www.youtube.com/watch?v=0oSGIC irVs</u>.[14]

There is another video that suggests it works: <u>https://www.youtube.com/watch?v=2uzXHnUViro</u>.[15]

It bothers me to think that other doctors and specialists have a different opinion than Dr. Fauci, and they can't be heard because their videos are taken down. They are being censored, but why? Could it be because hydroxychloroquine is a cheaper drug? This article left me with a bad feeling "(<u>Natural News</u>) On Dec. 20, an SCI Pharmtech manufacturing facility in Taoyuan City, Taiwan, <u>burst into flames and exploded</u>, leaving two people injured.

The facility, which manufactures <u>the anti-Wuhan coronavirus (COVID-19) drug hydroxychloroquine</u>, appears to have been targeted, perhaps by COVID-19 vaccine interests, in an effort to punish the company for manufacturing the inexpensive, highly effective remedy for the novel virus."[16] Do you think this a coincidence? Whatever happened to herd immunity?

Doctors then started using remdesivir with a combination of other medications that appeared to work. The problem was that our elderly and people with diabetes or other health issues were at higher risk of getting the virus. President Trump sadly contracted the virus and had to go to Walter Reed Hospital. He said in a briefing that he was given an experimental drug called regeneron, remdesivir, and a steroid. A couple of days later, he was released from the hospital and said he felt great. It was also announced that First Lady Melania also contracted the virus. Today she is fine, but then it was announced that their son Barron also contracted the virus. He had mild symptoms and bounced back quickly. Our president said that he would make this drug free to us because it was not our fault that anyone caught this virus, and he would hold China accountable.

We have the mad man, as I call him, Bill Gates and Dr. Fauci pushing vaccines. I personally would not let either one of them give me a vaccine. I don't trust either one of them; that is just my personal opinion.

Here we go again. I got an automated call that our state has gone from a three to a ten on the scale for coronavirus cases, and we are in the red zone.

"A Centers for Disease Control <u>report</u> released in September shows that masks and face coverings are not effective in preventing the spread of COVID-19, even for those people who consistently wear them."[17]

Who do you consider to be more dangerous? a smart butt with a tweet or a dumb butt with a pen? Think about it. We might not have liked some of President Trump's tweets, but his policies were good. Then we have Biden with a pen undoing everything Trump did. The only reason he would do such a thing is out of spite or to get back into bed with China. Make no mistake China is an enemy of the US and they want to be the super power of the world.

For all of those that want a communist country, dictatorship, socialism or Marxism go live in one of those countries first before trying to bring it to the United States. Let's see if you still feel that way after living in one of these countries. Don't you get people leave these countries to move to the United States for the freedoms that we have.

Chapter 2

The Lock Downs

Other countries had strict lock downs where you could not leave your home. There was no one on the streets. It looked like a ghost town. The United States also had lock downs but not as strict. Our essential businesses were allowed to stay open. We could go to work if our jobs were not closed down. If your job was shut down, some were offered the opportunity to work from home or we got paid for being off. Others had to file for unemployment. Most people made more on unemployment than they did working so when it was time to go back to work some people did not want to go back. We could go to the store, pharmacy, hospital, doctors, or anything else considered essential but most doctors preferred you to do telephone conference or video conferences. Emergency rooms would only let the patient in (which means no loved one could enter the hospital with you.) Hospitals and nursing homes would not allow visitors. Could you imagine that there was no one there to advocate for their loved one or maybe you needed to have a major surgery and there was no one there for moral support. That had to be a very scary feeling. All dine- in restaurants were closed in the beginning and when they did open back up, there had to be a six feet space between patrons. You could always go to the drive up for fast food because they were considered essential worker but all workers in any business had to wear mask. This was the silliest thing because you can't eat with a mask covering your face and who knows how far the virus can really travel. Churches were closed even though the churches offered alternatives, for example they offered outside services which were not accepted in some areas, they offered a drive- in style type church or virtual church. Some Pastors were arrested for continuing to hold church services. I felt this was a violation of our first amendment to close down the churches.

The Supreme Court believes in the Constitution and has enforced it. "It is time—past time—to make plain" that the Constitution applies at all times, even in pandemics. "'In a 5-4 vote late on Wednesday evening, the Supreme Court issued an injunction against Governor Andrew Cuomo's order that allowed businesses to operate at the capacity of their choosing but limited religious services to either 10 or 25 people at a time." [1]

Schools were closed down which was hard on the children. Some of those children relied on the free lunch program. Children were not allowed to socialize, despite the science saying that children are less likely to contract covid-19. This should have ticked people off because you had Nancy, Biden and Fauci running around saying trust the science but that was when it was convenient for them. The children had to do virtual learning which was hard on parents that had to work or had more than one child because you had to sit there with your child while they connected to their classroom via their iPAD but what about the families that could not afford iPADS or computers? It was hard on parents that had no idea what their child was doing in school due to language barriers, or parents that were not able to help their child due to illness. The children were not really learning much with this method. Children could not have birthday parties so they had driven by birthday parties where people would drive by and honk their horns. It was not the same as having your family and friends over. The same could be said for those that were graduating from high school or college. They did not get to walk down that isle and receive there diploma and there were no open houses and big celebrations. The beaches and parks were closed which just looked wrong. All my life I have always seen families at the beach and park and now nothing.

It is kind of crazy that churches had to close but liquor stores, marijuana dispensaries and smoke shops could stay open because they were considered essential businesses. This was the time that people needed God the most. Businesses in my state would not allow you entry unless you were wearing a mask. I found this to be unconstitutional as well because if you are carrying a fire arm you are not supposed to be wearing a mask. You could go to the grocery store but they had lines everywhere, to make sure that you would be six feet apart. Everything was just a mess and inconvenient. South Dakota never closed their state down and they seemed to do well. I wonder if it had something to do with the herd immunity. That is another issue some doctors had disagreements on. Think about it, when we had the N1H1 it was also a respiratory virus but we never had to wear any mask, in fact the Obama administration ordered the states to stop testing. All we heard from Dr. Fauci, Nancy Pelosi and Joe Biden was trusting the science but even scientist disagree. It was like the American people had no say so any more, on where they went and what they did. Everything was decided for you.

The part that really irritated me about the whole mask thing and everyone saying mask work is that they released people from jail and prison early because of the pandemic but if the mask really worked, why not leave them in jail or prison with their mask?

One funny thing about some of the stores is that you had to go in one door and could only exit through another door. It reminds me of something my brother said to me. He said "I don't think the corona virus cares which door you go in and exit from." I got a good laugh out of that one. At least we found some humor in this mess.

The lock downs led to other problems. It led to more people abusing alcohol and drugs. It led to suicides. It led to more physical abuse and sexual abuse. Could you imagine being locked in your home with an abuser? They had no place to go, but of course they had hot lines but what good is it when you have nowhere to run? How could you even have a private conversation in your own home with the one that is abusing you?

They are closing down the schools and government offices. This occurred 11-16-2020. Walmart is still open and other businesses at this current time. We cannot afford to shut down this economy again and the President said that we will not be closing it down.

We had people in financial crisis and the government came up with an idea of a stimulas package called the Cares Act. "In March 2020, U.S. lawmakers agreed on the passage of a $2 trillion stimulus bill called the <u>CARES (Coronavirus Aid, Relief, and Economic Security) Act</u> to blunt the impact of an economic downturn set in motion by the global coronavirus pandemic. On March 27, 2020, President Trump signed the bill into law." With most forecasters predicting that the U.S. economy is either already in a recession or heading into one, policymakers crafted legislation that dedicates historic government funding to support large and small businesses, industries, individuals and families, gig workers and independent contractors, and hospitals." This was the breakdown of the Cares Act:

- $367 billion loan and grant program for small businesses
- Expansion of unemployment benefits to include people <u>furloughed</u>, gig workers, and freelancers, with benefits increased by $600 per week for a period of four months
- Direct payments to families of $1,200 per adult and $500 per child for households making up to $75,000
- Over $130 billion to hospitals, health care systems, and providers
- $500 billion fund for loans to corporate America (which Democrats called a <u>slush fund</u> when the Treasury was solely in charge) overseen by an inspector general and a congressional panel, with every loan document made public
- Cash grants of $25 billion for airlines (in addition to loans), $4 billion for air cargo carriers, $3 billion for airline contractors (caterers, etc.) for payroll support
- Ban on stock buybacks for large companies receiving government loans during the term of their assistance plus one year
- $150 billion to state and local governments [2]

The democrats and republicans went back and forth on the amounts until they finally reached an agreement. Some politicians care about the American people but for the most part it seems to be a game of war between democrats and republicans.

The second stimulus package was going to be called the Heroes Act but Nancy Pelosi wanted an absurd amount and once again she made it political. She did not care about the American people just her own agenda. The President stated that this was to be for the American people but good old Nancy wanted money for Assistance to state and local governments. The President was not going to allow money to go to democrat cities that allowed all the crazy rioting, looting, vandalism, murders, and other crimes that destroyed their cities and rightfully so. Why would anyone give money to those that broke their oath to defend and protect their cities and allow them to be destroyed? Nancy wanted another $600 per person on unemployment due to the corona virus but we already seen the problem this caused the president was offering an additional $400 per week to those on unemployment. She wanted $25 billion for the Postal Service and 3.6 billion for election security. [3] Now I understand why the President calls her crazy Nancy. Her demeanor changed when she was in front of the cameras however she put on the loving and caring show. She said it was all about the American people and blamed republicans and the President of course. She never mentioned her crazy demands.

In reality she was just playing a game with the "Heroes Act" She never intended for it to pass because she did not want to make the President look good before the election and the President tweeted out to her that he was ready to sign a bill for the people.

"It's been eight months since Congress passed their stimulus package, the CARES Act. As the COVID-19 pandemic continues to pose a grave problem for those in the United States, Americans have been wondering whether Congress will be able to negotiate another package. According to CNBC, Treasury Secretary Steven Mnuchin recently said that he, along with other GOP leaders, will try to draft another stimulus bill with Democrats in the upcoming weeks." [4]

Nancy does not care that people are applying for public assistance and standing in line at food banks. People cannot afford to pay their bills. She does not need to worry about money living in her seven-million-dollar mansion while others suffer. This is all about Nancy getting her way and making the President look bad.

"In a Fox News interview Monday, the former South Carolina congressman and federal prosecutor teed off on the Democratic House speaker after Pelosi admitted last week that she's open to passing a realistic coronavirus relief package now because she expects former Vice President Joe Biden to be sworn in to the presidency in January.

It was a sharp change from recent months, when Pelosi and her Democratic colleagues insisted on measures, they knew were unacceptable to Republicans in a transparent effort to delay federal aid to Americans to hurt President Donald Trump at the voting booth." [5] I told you Nancy was just playing politics.

"I can tell you Mark Meadows and I will be speaking with Mitch McConnell and Kevin McCarthy this morning," Manuchin said. "And we are going to come up with a plan to sit down with Pelosi and Schumer and try to get a targeted bill done for the people that really need it. And hopefully the Democrats will work with us." McConnell also released a statement on Friday about stimulus negotiations in which he noted that Republicans are in support of enacting another package. [6] We have three days until Thanksgiving how many American people are going to do without a Thanksgiving dinner? Then you have the hypocritical governor form California. "Right now, Gavin Newsom is leading one of the dumbest, most anti-science corona virus responses in the nation as his state continues to set records for total infections, and not content with the current lack of progress, the governor decided to just go with a full dystopian nightmare for the holidays." [7] "California Gov. <u>Gavin Newsom</u> (D) has found himself in the same hot water that House Speaker Nancy Pelosi (D-Calif.) was in after her <u>hair salon trip</u> this summer, in his case for a dinner at Napa County's ultra-exclusive French Laundry restaurant that bucked the tenor of his own COVID-19 safety advice."[8]

What hypocracy one rule for them and another for the rest of us." There was no social distancing, no mask and twelve or more people.

Nancy Pelosci strikes me as a woman that cannot take responsibility for her own actions and she was playing politics with people's lives. She did not want people to get the stimulus checks under Trump because she did not want to do anything to make him look good to the American people and she thought that if the receive checks under Trump it would help him win re-election.

I have also learned with the Biden administration, if anything goes wrong just blame Trump whether he did it or not or whether he was in office or not.

Chapter 3

Dr. Fauci

D r. Fauci, "is an American physician and <u>immunologist</u> who has served as the director of the <u>National Institute of Allergy and Infectious Diseases</u> (NIAID) since 1984. Since January 2020, he has been one of the lead members of the <u>Trump administration's</u> <u>White House Coronavirus Task Force</u> addressing the <u>COVID-19 pandemic in the United States</u>. Dr. Fauci was also a scientist and worked for NIH."[1]

This is the same man that lied to us in the beginning saying that we did not need to wear mask but later said that we did need to wear mask and claims he only said we did not need them because there was a shortage for health care workers. Why didn't he just tell us the truth from the beginning and tell us to make homemade mask. That is what people ended up doing any ways.

Dr. Fauci told us over and over to wear a mask, social distance, and wash our hands. He repeated it so much that you could hear it in your sleep. He is the same man that does not even practice what he preaches. Remember he was caught sitting next to two friends at a game without wearing his mask. People really started to lose faith in him and some did not even want to see or hear from him anymore. He keeps saying that we are heading for a second wave of covid-19 only time will tell. He wants to close down the economy but people are tired of this and they just want to go back to work and return to normal. He claims we will not see normal for a while in fact it could way into 2022. It seems like he is always on television or some media reporters are talking about what Dr. Fauci on the nightly news.

"Anthony Fauci Plotted 'Global Vaccine Action Plan'
with Bill Gates Before Pushing COVID Panic and
Doubts About Hydroxychloroquine Treatments."[2]

"Fauci: No scientific evidence the coronavirus was made in a Chinese lab"[3]

We do know that it was really made in a lab in China because Dr Li-Meng Yan a virologist that was working on the virus in Wuhan, China came forward and told us. So these are just some of the reasons I have issues and concerns about Anthony Fauci. It kind of appears that he is making this political and maybe for his own gain.

Dr. Fauci did not want the truth to come out but it did. "Judicial Watch announced that it and the Daily Caller News Foundation received 301 pages of emails of Dr. Anthony Fauci from the U.S. Department of Health and Human Services showing that National Institutes of Health (NIH) officials tailored confidentiality forms to China's terms and that the World Health Organization (WHO) conducted an unreleased, strictly confidential Covid-19 epidemiological analysis in January 2020." "These new emails show the WHO and Fauci's NIH special accommodations to Chinese communist efforts to control information about Covid-19," said Judicial Watch President Tom Fitton.

The emails, obtained by Judicial Watch via a Freedom of Information Act (FOIA) lawsuit, "set the tone early on in the coronavirus outbreak. It's clear that the WHO allowed China to control the information flow from the start."[4] Now the ugly truth begins to rear its ugly head. Personally, I feel like Fauci should have criminal charges pressed against him and crimes against humanity and his friend Bill Gates too. I suspect that we will receive more information on Dr. Fauci and his intent. There is a scripture in the Bible that says once that was in the dark will come to light.

The next time I hear Dr. Fauci scream trust the science I am going to run in the other direction. This man is a scientist and had a duty to be honest with the American people but chose not to.

I mentioned earlier that we would never know how many human beings really perished from covid 19 and here is why: MONDAY, April 20, 2020 (HealthDay News) — The United States first coronavirus tests were ineffective due to poor laboratory practices at the U.S. Centers for Disease Control and <u>Prevention</u>, the U.S. Food and Drug Administration said.

"The CDC's own manufacturing standards were violated by two of the agency's three labs in Atlanta that created the coronavirus test kits. As a result, the CDC sent ineffective tests to nearly all of the 100 state and local public health labs, according to the FDA, *The New York Times* reported."[5]

People were stressed out and paranoid. They were so paranoid that they were driving with their mask on, bike riding with their mask on, and walking with their mask on. This is not normal. I have one friend that barely left her house. She ordered her groceries off line and everything else she needed. This cannot be mentally or physically healthy. Can you imagine living in constant fear?

I mention earlier that we may never know the true number of covid 19 deaths and this is why "Dr. Jensen then told Laura Ingraham of FOX news that under the CDC guidelines, a patient who died after being hit by a bus and tested positive for coronavirus would be listed as having presumed to have died from the virus regardless of whatever damage was caused by the bus."[6] This should be considered fraud. From the same Fox show I heard the rest of the disturbing story "Right now Medicare has determined that if you have a COVID-19 admission to the hospital you'll get paid $13,000. If that COVID-19 patient goes on a ventilator, you get $39,000; three times as much." "Some physicians really have a bent towards public health and they will put down influenza or whatever because that's their preference, Jensen added. I try to stay very specific, very precise. If I know I've got pneumonia, that's what's going on the death certificate. I'm not going to add stuff just because it's convenient."[7] He was just one of the honest doctors but what about the ones that are not so honest?

What about hospitals receiving so much money for admissions of covid and for those put-on ventilators? This could really corrupt the medical field.

Dr. Fauci says that mask work. Is there a scientific study saying that masks work? "Did you hear about the peer-reviewed study done by Stanford University that demonstrates beyond a reasonable doubt that face masks have absolutely zero chance of preventing the spread of Covid-19? No? It was posted on the National Center for Biotechnological Information government website. The NCBI is a branch of the National Institute for Health, so one would think such a study would be widely reported by mainstream media and embraced by the "science-loving" folks in Big Tech."[8]

Dr. Fauci says social distancing works. Are there any scientific studies on social distancing? "New research has cast doubt on the "six-foot rule" that has informed social distancing guidelines used around the world during the COVID-19 pandemic.

"Massachusetts Institute of Technology (MIT) professors Martin Z. Bazant and John W.M. Bush have challenged the long-held guideline adopted by the US Centers for Disease Control and Prevention and the World Health Organisation.

They claim the risk of being exposed to the virus indoors is the same at 60 feet as six feet – even while wearing a mask."

"The six-foot rule, the researchers argue, is largely based on an outdated belief that the biggest risk is so-called large drop transmission directly from the mouth of an infected person, whereas there is now overwhelming evidence that airborne transmission through microdroplets held aloft on-air currents actually plays the dominant role in the spread of COVID-19."

That means the six-foot rule offers little protection from virus-bearing aerosol droplets that are sufficiently small to be continuously mixed through an indoor space.[9]

Dr. Fauci believed in the lock downs. Is there a scientific study proving lock downs work?[10] "Studies since March 2020 have documented and assessed the impacts of mass quarantining of healthy populations, a policy never attempted before in modern medicine. A precept in medicine is ***first do no harm***, but lockdowns are proven to do much harm for little or no good. Below we cite 27 published papers finding that lockdowns had little or no efficacy (despite unconscionable harms) along with a key quote or two from each. (10)" You can follow the link provided to read the full article. (https://principia-scientific.com/so-far-27-studies-prove-lockdowns-have-little-to-no-effect/).

Dr. Fauci is not God but some people listen to him like he preaches the gospel. The man had his own agenda. He failed the American people in my opinion and I know I will be criticized for saying so especially by some news media stations, big tech and big pharma but I need to get the truth out there. Please do your own research on everything and trust no one.

It seems like when the cameras are off so is Dr. Fauci's mask.

Why is Bill Gates sending emails to Dr. Fauci? Why is Zuckerberg sending emails to Fauci?

Chapter 4

The Murder Of George Floyd

All Americans watched in horror as a white police officer held his knee against the neck of a black man named George Floyd for almost nine minutes as Mr. Floyd said several times he could not breathe and cried out for his mama with two other officers present one asked should we get him up and the one with his knee to Mr. Floyds neck said no. Bystanders we recording this horrific scene on their cell phones but no one stepped into to help Mr. Floyd. Later it came out that Mr. Floyd had a criminal past but that is no excuse for his murder and that is how I perceived it. Later on, the officers were charged and a tape was released that Mr. Floyd took some type of drug before the incident occurred. I don't know what type of drug he took and it really does not matter. The officer used excessive force. He had other officers on the scene to assist him and they could have put him in the back of the squad car once he was subdued and handcuffed. There was no reason that I could see for the abuse of power.

I was not the only one outraged at this blatant abuse of power. Now this took place in May of 2020 in Minneapolis, Minnesota. People had the right to be mad and they started protesting in Minneapolis and rightfully so. At first the protest was peaceful and the protest even went nationwide and at some point, Black Lives Matter got involved. Eventually the protest led to violence, looting, rioting, and more murders. Businesses were destroyed and even burnt to the ground. Protesters threw whatever they could at police officers. I thought of Dr. Martin Luther King a man that I admired. I thought if only he were alive, he would be telling these folks, no violence. He had an effective way of getting his point across without the violence and it made no sense at all to burn down businesses in your own community. The National Guard finally had to be called in.

Even though I only witnessed three officers at the scene on all the news channels they said a couple of days later those four officers had been fired and charged. I don't know where the fourth officer was at the time perhaps, I was too focused on the officer's knee on the neck of Mr. Floyd.

By no means do I think all police officers are bad because I have met a few good ones in my life time but we have had problems with police officers abusing their power in just about every state. The news media does not help either. Sometimes I feel they are a part of the problem. They repeated this story over and over but yet if a white officer killed a white person there was no mention of it. Another example was when a black man walked up and shot a five-year-old boy the media barely covered that story. I can only imagine how heartbroken those parents were. They will probably never recover from the death of their son. When a black officer was murdered, they barely mentioned him. I don't understand why. That officer had a wife and children. He had a family that loved him.

Protests began in Seattle, Washington. The Mayor Jenny Durkan claimed that the protests were peaceful but I am not sure what channel she was watching because all I saw was violence on the news. You had the rioting, looting, vandalism and violence. The protesters even took over part of the city at first, they called their turf CHOP but later changed the name to CHAZ and you had Mayor Jenny Durkan saying you could call it the summer of love. Is this Mayor insane? If this is her idea of love, I would be terrified to see how she interprets hate. Here goes the hypocracy. Later she had to call in the National Guard. She really made herself look bad to the American people.

"Portland, Oregan - a demonstration in Portland, Oregon, that included people breaking windows and taking down statues of former Presidents Theodore Roosevelt and Abraham Lincoln has been declared a riot by police."[1]

"In early September, protesters hurled multiple fire bombs, mortars, rocks and other items and police officers on the 100th night of demonstrations in the city, Hundreds of protesters have been arrested by authorities in Portland since late May, according to AP." President Trump signed an executive order punishing anyone destroying statues with a prison term of up to 10 years.

These government officials take an oath to serve and protect their cities but there is something terribly wrong when they start committing crimes against America. Sen. Louise Lucas faces charges of conspiracy to commit a felony and injury to a monument in excess of $1,000, Portsmouth Police Chief Angela Greene said during a news conference. The protest occurred in June. Senator Louise Lucas did turn herself in.[2]

Lucas is a longtime Democratic legislator and a key power broker in the state Senate, joining the chamber in 1992. The charges were filed the same week Virginia lawmakers are taking up dozens of criminal justice reforms during a special legislative session.[3] Do you see the hypocracy? The very people that should be fighting crime are engaging in it. We should all be afraid to go to sleep at night with people like this around. These people are not making the best decisions for American people. What ever happened to loving one another? What has happened to humanity?

Soon we started hearing chants do defund the police. Whose dumb idea was that? The people do not want to defund the police so that means the representatives that we voted for are not even considering what the people want. This has all turned into a political war.

Who did they think they were going to call in case of emergency? The Ghost Busters!

We also had a crazy bunch of protesters called Antifa that some just dismissed as an ideology and not an organization. I got news for you they are an organization, they sued Judicial Watch. "(**Washington, DC**) — Judicial Watch announced that a U.S. District Judge in California awarded Judicial Watch $22,000 in legal fees in a case filed by an Antifa organizer in an effort to block Judicial Watch from obtaining information about her activities."

I remember Nadler saying Antifa did not exist.

"Yvette Felarca, a middle school teacher in the Berkeley Unified School District (BUSD), and two co-plaintiffs were ordered to pay Judicial Watch $22,000 in attorney's fees and $4,000 in litigation costs. Felarca had <u>sued</u> the BUSD in federal court to keep the school district from fulfilling its legal obligation to provide Judicial Watch with records of their communications mentioning: Felarca, Antifa, and/or BAMN. Judicial Watch also asked for Felarca's personnel file. Felarca is a prominent figure in <u>By Any Means Necessary</u> (BAMN), a group founded by the Marxist Revolutionary Workers League that protests conservative speaking engagements. In 2016, Felarca and two of her allies were arrested and charged with several crimes, including felony assault, for inciting a riot in Sacramento. Earlier this year, Felarca was ordered to <u>stand trial</u> for assault."[4]

That means that they have their own attorneys and to add fuel to the fire they were organized enough to have someone deliver their supplies and riot gear, weapons, signs and water. Antifa has been around for a long time and are in my opinion paid protesters and the reason for false chaos. This video shows antifa wanting their money from George Soros[5] https://www.youtube.com/watch?v=QpPS9IWXSa4

"Paid liberal protesters totally exist; it's an excellent career choice with surprisingly good benefits; and each protester earns $1,500 a week.)"[6]

George Soros always denies his involvement but he has been involved across the globe not just in the United States. A paid protester that comes forward and lets us know he is getting paid from Mr. George Soros. Watch this video:[7] https://www.youtube.com/watch?v=op1yqcIdhbE.

It is a tragedy that David Dorn did not get as much recognition as George Floyd. David Dorn was a hero. Chief Hayden said Dorn had been a fine captain who had been very well-liked and looked up to by many of the department's younger officers. Dorn had been killed around 2:30 a.m. Tuesday, dying on the sidewalk in front of the pawn store he had been providing security for. Dorn's son Brian Powell told the station that Dorn had been a father of five and had 10 grandchildren. President Donald Trump also paid tribute to Dorn on Twitter, saying, "Our highest respect to the family of David Dorn, a Great Police Captain from St. Louis, who was viciously shot and killed by despicable looters last night. We honor our police officers, perhaps more than ever before. Thank you!"[8] This man was loved by his family, friends, and community. His life mattered just as much as George Floyd.

"We cannot forget about Black Lives Matter (BLM). It is important to understand where BLM gets its funding "Billionaire investor George Soros has donated millions of dollars to Black Lives Matter through his Open Society Foundation, according to the Washington Times."[9]

"Black Lives Matter co-founder Patrisse Cullors said in a newly surfaced video from 2015 that she and her fellow organizers are trained Marxists – making clear their movement's ideological foundation, according to a report."[10]

We might want to point out that the BLM organization only seemed to focus on white police officers killing black men or women. They did not concentrate on blacks killing blacks or black children getting killed. They did not seem to focus on black businesses being destroyed by vandalism, looting, and burnt to the ground so it makes me curious as to why they call themselves Black Lives Matter when that really does not appear to be the cause. Shouldn't all black lives matter? Do you see the hypocrisy? Where was BLM while black children were being murdered? When you hear the term Black Lives Matter you think that all Black Lives would matter to the organization but that is not the case. Do you see the hypocrisy with the name Black Lives Matter?

Now here is an interesting twist. "Rashad Turner, a former BLM leader, says he quit the group after realizing it doesn't care about helping black families." In a YouTube video called "the truth revealed about BLM", he said: "In 2015, I was the founder of Black Lives Matter in St. Paul.

"I believed the organization stood for exactly what the name implies – black lives matter."

"However, after a year on the inside, I learned they had little concern for rebuilding black families."

"He said BLM "cared even less about improving the quality of education for students in Minneapolis, adding it was made clear when they publicly denounced charter schools alongside the teachers' union".[11] This man is a man to be admired he found out the ugly truth and changed things up to make them right.

BLM should have been protesting for all the innocent black children that were killed in the senseless mess. They should have been doing things to strengthen the black communities, not destroying them. They should have been encouraging the family unit staying together. They should have been trying to put an end to all the violence and the black-on-black killings. They should have been fighting for school choice. Instead, they only focused on black men getting killed by white officers. They should have been acknowledging the black officers that lost their lives to these riots. They sure could learn a history lesson from Dr. Martin Luther King. He is probable rolling over in his grave right now with disappointment.

Chapter 5

The Media

What ever happened to good investigative reporting? We have very few left. There contempt for our President seems to be the only thing that they can focus on. It is really disappointing that they can't even report on anything else. There are murders occurring every day and they don't report on them or they will mention them briefly and then you never hear any more about it. Another thing they report on daily is the corona virus. I think we could all use a break from that. It is the same thing day after day. I understand why the President calls them the fake news. They try to instill fear into the American people and they only tell half-truths, no truth at all or show only half videos that fit their narrative.

Since when do the media call presidential elections? MSN and other main stream media called the race for 2020. It is not up to them. The New York Post made a comment about VP Pence and the President being in the rain at the Arlington Cemetery laying a wreath while their wives were covered with umbrellas. Seriously the man can't do anything without scrutiny. I remember he made a joke at a press conference about injecting disinfectant and the press ate it up. They totally distorted the joke then you had commercials coming on saying please do not inject bleach or any other disinfectant. Notice there is a connection between the media and politicians or people in power. Take a look at the list below to get an idea of the corruption and what drives them.

Seriously you morons need to get a life.

- "ABC News President Ben Sherwood, who is the brother of Elizabeth Sherwood-Randall, a top national-security adviser to President Obama.
- His counterpart at CBS, news division president David Rhodes, is the brother of Benjamin Rhodes, a key foreign-policy specialist.
- CNN's deputy Washington bureau chief, Virginia Moseley, is married to Tom Nides, who until earlier this year was deputy secretary of state under Hillary Rodham Clinton.
- White House press secretary Jay Carney's wife is Claire Shipman, a veteran reporter for ABC.
- NPR's White House correspondent, Ari Shapiro, is married to a lawyer, Michael Gottlieb, who joined the White House counsel's office in April.
- The *Post*'s Justice Department reporter, Sari Horwitz, is married to William B. Schultz, the general counsel of the Department of Human Services.
- [VP] Biden's current communications director, Shailagh Murray (a former *Post* congressional reporter), is married to Neil King, one of the *Wall Street Journal*'s top political reporters.

This list doesn't even include those dating and sleeping together."[1]

Claire Shipman is married to former Whitehouse Press Secretary Jay Carney

 ABC News and Univision reporter Matthew Jaffe is married to Katie Hogan, Obama's Deputy Press Secretary

 ABC President Ben Sherwood is the brother of Obama's Special Adviser Elizabeth Sherwood

WONDER WHY MEDIA COVERS TRUMP UNFAIRLY?

DAVID RHODES	BEN RHODES	BEN SHERWOOD	LIZ SHERWOOD	VIRGINIA MOSELEY	TOM NIDES
PRESIDENT CBS	OBAMA STAFF	FMR ABC PRESIDENT	OBAMA STAFF	CNN DEPUTY CHIEF	HILLARY STAFF

 BROTHERS   SIBLINGS   MARRIED

 CBS NEWS  abc NEWS   CNN

People rely on the news and think that they are getting the truth from the main stream media but that just is not so in reality. Most of the media are bias and for Joe Biden. Most reporters can't wait to condemn our President, twist his words or just print false stories. It is only hurting them in the long run because people are waking up. The media and their corruption are being exposed. They are becoming an enemy to the people.

The twist in the story is that they will do anything to cover up for Joe Biden and his crime family as I call them. When Hunter

Biden's lap top was left in a repair shop in Delaware the owner was disturbed by what he saw on it, in fact he was so disturbed he made several copies and gave two to friends in case he was murdered. He finally ended up giving a copy to Rudy Giuliani, after he said he already gave a copy to the FBI but never heard any more about it. It turns out that the FBI has had an ongoing investigation into Hunter Biden and the Biden family for money laundering since 2019. Here is what the New York Times had to say "President Trump's allies have promoted claims of corruption aimed at the former vice president's son in an effort to damage the Biden campaign." They did not seem to care about the crimes that were on the lap top they just seemed to be protecting sleepy Joe. The New York Post was the first ones to break the story but from what I understand they were censored by Twitter and Facebook.

I would advise everyone to watch the youtube video about Google, Facebook, and twitter. https://www.youtube.com/watch?v=hAZphlEzPNc.[3] On October 28, 2020 Big Tech appeared before congress to answer question about the censoring. Section 230 gave these big tech companies protection from liability for what their users post. Twitter was blocking the New York Post story claiming it was hacked material but the hypocracy here is that they allowed some one the right to post President Trump's taxes on line which was illegal. See the hypocracy. Twitter was also locking a lot of people out of their accounts around election time. They locked Kayleigh McEnany the Presidents press secretary out of her account and she is a decent human being but yet they did not lock AOC out of her account with her crazy tweets.

Facebook uses fact checkers but who checks the fact checkers? I posted and article on facebook from the CDC website and they said my post was partly false. How can it be partly false if it came from the CDC?

Like I mentioned before they were and still are protected by 230 so they should not be censoring anyone unless the post is violent or threatening.

Candace Owens is not a woman to mess with and the fact

checkers from face book are about to find out. "Candace Owens, a conservative activist touted by President Trump, announced she has filed a lawsuit against independent fact-checkers that Facebook uses to flag misinformation."[4]

"It is time to fact-check the fact-checkers," Ms. Owens said in the video. "I'm sick of this. I'm sick of the censorship. It's wrong. It's disgusting, the activist added."[5] Watch the video (https://www.foxnews.com/politics/candace-owens-targets-facebook-3rd-party-fact-checkers-with-lawsuit) Candace Owens is just one of my favorite people and I hope she brings facebook to their knees it seems like they have gotten too big for their britches. They forgot who supported and who made them, once they reached the big time.

One thing that President Trump and Joe Biden both agree on is repealing section 230.

I am telling you know if they can censor the politicians, they can censor you too. They are violating our right to free speech and suppressing facts from us.

Apparently, you can't mention George Soros on the news either: "This past week Newt Gingrich was on FOX and he talked about the fact that George Soros gave massive financial backing to radical leftists who ran for district attorney in various states, and Gingrich basically got shut down by some of the network hosts."[6] Well, I must double down on this one.

"Anti-American George Soros was interviewed by 60 Minutes years ago. In this infamous interview Soros claimed to have no shame for turning in fellow Jews to the Nazis in World War II Hungary. The Nazis stole from the Jews and Soros claimed that if he didn't do it, someone else would."[7] This is the man many believe is behind today's modern corrupt Democrat Party: "Soros was reportedly behind the airport protests after President Trump's election. A week before that Soros was reportedly behind 50 Groups involved in the Women's Protests the day after the inauguration. Before that, Soros was connected to the groups demanding election recounts after the November 8th election and Soros money was funding more protests during these efforts. And there was information showing that <u>Soros funded Black Lives Matter</u> protests across the country. **We also have reported** that far left billionaire George Soros has been systematically targeting district attorney races throughout the United States. Many of his backed candidates have won their races and are causing havoc across the country."[8]

"US Attorney General Bill Barr spoke with Martha MacCallum on FOX News. Bill Barr called out George Soros for subverting the legal system in the US and creating more crime and violence."[9]

Do you see the way politicians use the media, the media uses politics and big tech and George Soros play their parts? It is all to keep Americans from learning the truth and violating our rights. Really, they are taking them away slowly and have been for some time.

In my opinion, they are trying to keep us so distracted by the virus, riots, censoring, fake news and their games so that we can't really focus on what is truly happening in congress.

It is better to understand who is related to whom and then it becomes clearer as to why we have bias reporters.

Reporters should always report the facts and the facts only so that the American people can make informed decisions.

Speaking of decisions, we should have all been able to make decisions for ourselves on whether we wanted to wear a mask or not. It is our body and our choice. That is one of the arguments that they have used for abortions for years so that same logic should apply to us in this scenario.

Chapter 6

Scandals And Corruption

This is what Senator Lindsy Graham had to say about Crossfire Hurricane "I consider the Crossfire Hurricane investigation a massive system failure by senior leadership, but not representative of the dedicated, hardworking patriots who protect our nation every day at Federal Bureau of Investigation and the Department of Justice. I believe that Crossfire Hurricane was one of the most incompetent and corrupt investigations in the history of the FBI and DOJ."

"The FISA court was lied to. Exculpatory information was withheld on those being investigated. The investigators, with some notable exceptions, were incredibly biased and used the powers of law enforcement for political purposes. The subjects of the investigation had their lives turned upside down. It is my hope that counterintelligence investigations will be reined in and this never happens again in America.

"The leadership of the FBI under Comey and McCabe was either grossly incompetent or they knowingly allowed tremendous misdeeds. There was a blind eye turned toward any explanation other than the Trump campaign was colluding with foreign powers. At every turn the FBI and DOJ ran stop signs that were in abundance regarding exculpatory information."

The FISA warrant applications against Carter Page were a travesty, and those who signed them have acknowledged that if they knew then what they know now, they would not have signed it.

It is hard to believe that the senior officials at the FBI did not know that the Steele Dossier had been disavowed by the Russian subsource. It is equally hard to believe that the warnings from the CIA and other agencies about the reliability of Christopher Steele and the dossier were not known to senior leadership. It is my hope that the Durham report will hold those accountable for the travesty called Crossfire Hurricane.

"There was no 'there' there. The investigation was pushed when it should have been stopped and the only logical explanation is that the investigators wanted an outcome because of their bias."[1]

The Impeachment of President Donald Trump or should I say a scam, one of the most outrageous things the left has done since spying on him before he became president. He was acquitted in February of 2020. The hypocracy here is that the Democrats wanted him out so bad that they spent three years trying to impeach the President with our tax dollars and they knew this was a bogus impeachment. They knew that they could not bully or bribe him. These are some sick individuals and if they can do this to the President of the United States, they can do it to you too.

Then we had the Harvey Weinstein scandal, Weinstein was accused of sexual harassment and touching women inappropriately. It came out that he paid some of these women to keep quiet. This went on for years after all he was in the perfect position to commit these disgusting acts.

"Harvey Weinstein was sentenced to 23 years and because of this case, it caused women to start the me-too movement. This movement encourages women to speak out about sexual abuse."[2]

"Then we had the stock market crash of 2020. Our economy was doing very well under the Trump administration until the corona virus hit, then things went spiraling down. The stock market crash of 2020 began on Monday, March 9, with history's largest point plunge for the Dow Jones Industrial Average (DJIA) up to that date. It was followed by two more record-setting point drops on March 12 and

March 16. The stock market crash included the three worst point drops in U.S. history."[3] It did not take us long to make a comeback but we are still not where we were before the crash.

The Black Lives Matter (BLM) protest began over the death of George Floyd. I mention in an earlier chapter that a black man named George Floyd was killed by a white police officer holding his knee on George Floyd's neck for almost nine minutes. Everyone was outraged of all colors and religions. Something like this should have never happened. I know the officers were fired and charged but are still awaiting trial. This sparked the protest of BLM which were peaceful protest in the beginning but it was not acceptable when they wanted to defund the police, this was not a good strategy since most neighborhoods want more police in their neighborhood. I really want people to understand that their protest has been rather peaceful until you started seeing Antifa and paid protesters show up that is really when the violence started with rioting, looting, and more murders. I do how ever have a problem with the name of BLM the name itself should mean all black lives matter but that was not the case. They have not protested any of the black children that have been killed, they have not protested any black officers being killed, and they don't protest black on black killings. The name contradicts itself.

BLM was started in 2013 by three black activists: Alicia Garza, Patrice Cullors, and Opal Tometi.

"The movement aims to eradicate white supremacy and dismantle systemic racism.

The women wanted to create a Black-centered political will and movement in response to the shooting death of <u>Florida</u> teenager <u>Trayvon Martin</u> in 2012.".[4]

We discussed Antifa in an earlier chapter but I just wanted to give you an overview of what they believe in. "Individuals involved in the antifa movement tend to hold <u>anti-authoritarian</u>,[39] <u>anticapitalist</u>,[40][41] <u>anti-fascist</u>,[42] and <u>anti-state</u> views,[10] subscribing to a varied range of <u>left-wing</u> ideologies.[43] A majority of adherents are <u>anarchists</u>, <u>communists</u>, and other <u>socialists</u> who describe themselves as <u>revolutionaries</u>,<u>[9]</u> although some <u>social democrats</u> and others on the <u>American Left</u>."[5]

We had the Jeffrey Epstein scandal in which Jeffrey Epstein has been accused of having sex with under aged girls and providing girls and boys for his friends. Most pod casters refer to his island as Pedo Island and he had a lot of prominent figures visiting his isle and riding on his private plane.

Ghislaine Maxwell was arrested some say she was Jeffrey Epstein's girlfriend and some say she was his pimp that procured underage girls and groomed them to have sex with Jeffrey and other famous clients. Some have even claimed she was Bill Clinton's girlfriend and there are pictures of the two together. "A Manhattan-born woman has claimed that she was gagged, restrained and raped by Ghislaine Maxwell — before Jeffrey Epstein joined in on the attack, according to an interview published Sunday."[6] "Maxwell, 58, was arrested in July and charged <u>on several counts</u> related to sex trafficking minors and perjury. She has pleaded not guilty in that case. She has previously denied the allegations against her, including under sworn testimony."[7] Jeffrey Epstein, they say committed suicide in his cell.

When I first heard of the Beirut explosion on the television the first to mind was a terrorist attack. Later I found that it was caused from ammonia nitrate that had been stored and exploded. "A massive <u>explosion ripped through</u> central Beirut on Tuesday, killing dozens of people, injuring thousands and blowing out windows in buildings across the city."

"The blast near Beirut's port sent up a huge mushroom cloud-shaped shockwave, flipping cars and damaging distant buildings. It was felt as far as Cyprus, hundreds of miles away, and registered as a 3.3 magnitude earthquake in the Lebanese capital."

"Lebanon's Prime Minister, Hassan Diab, said that 2,750 tons of ammonium nitrate, a highly explosive material used in fertilizers and bombs, <u>had been stored for six years at a port warehouse without safety measures</u>, endangering the safety of citizens, according to a statement."[8] They said on the news that the explosion made a huge mushroom shaped cloud. It reminds me of seeing atomic bombs on a television program my dad was watching when I was much younger.

The west coast wild fires were devastating and Joe Biden was blaming it on climate change but later I saw a video that showed people deliberately starting the fires. "California and Oregon in particular are far behind stated goals of treating millions of acres of forests and wild lands through restoration projects, selective thinning of trees and brush and prescribed burning."[9] It is hard to know what is true anymore with all the different theories. Some residents lost their homes and others were without power. Think of all the land burned up and all the wild life destroyed.

This year Judge Ruth Bader Ginsburg passed away. She served on the Supreme Court. She fought for gender equality and women's rights. She also fought for the Roe v. Wade case. "*Roe v. Wade* was a landmark legal decision issued on January 22, 1973, in which the U.S. Supreme Court struck down a Texas statute banning abortion, effectively legalizing the procedure across the United States. The court held that a woman's right to an abortion was implicit in the right to privacy protected by the 14th Amendment to the Constitution. Prior to *Roe v. Wade*, abortion had been illegal throughout much of the country since the late 19th century."[10] This case is or will be coming before the Supreme Court again sometime this year or next to rule it unconstitutional. I am pro-life so it will not bother me.

President Trump tested positive for Covid -19 and had to go to Walter Reed hospital where they used an experimental drug on him called regeneron. It seemed to work quickly because he was out of the hospital in a matter of days. The first lady Melania and their son also contracted covid -19. All seem to be doing well. The President said he felt good and was out campaigning the next week.

Oh, I can't forget we had the Presidential Election on November 3, 2020 and we still don't know who the President is. The media called it for Joe Biden but last time I checked they don't call elections. There are a lot of law suits going on and recounts right now because there were millions of mail- in- ballots that went out this year due to covid -19 and it has created a disaster. Dead people are voting, the voting machine had glitches, and you had people committing voter fraud. I don't know how long it will be before we know who the President of the United States is.

This year Eddie Van Halen and Sean Connery also passed away.

Today is November 15, 2020 so we don't have too much longer until this year is over with. It has been a rough year and, in some ways, also an awakening. I realized during the lock down that I need to be closer to God and that we often take things for granted. We complain about things that don't matter.

The bombshell of scandals was the Hunter Biden scandal. Little Mr. Hunter Biden left his lap top in a repair shop and never returned to pick it up. The repair shop owner was disturbed by the material on the lap top and called the FBI to give the copy but before giving the FBI a copy he made more copies and sent two of them to his friends in case he was murdered. He did not hear back from the FBI so he sent a copy to Rudy Giuliani. Come to find out the FBI had the lap top since 2019 and claimed they were looking into money laundering but they never came forward and told anyone during the impeachment trial of the President.

"A second laptop belonging to Hunter Biden was taken by the feds back in February.

The computer was found in the Massachusetts offices of celebrity psychiatrist Dr. Keith A blow during a raid and seized by Drug Enforcement Administration agents, according to a <u>new report from NBC</u>."

"Ablow's medical license was suspended after he was accused of sexually exploiting patients and other professional misconduct. He has not been charged with a crime and has denied the allegations. Hunter Biden has not been the target of the search or the investigation and his lawyer ultimately got the laptop back, the network reported."[11]

Hunter Biden's first lap top seemed to be the smoking gun that had pictures of him in the nude and smoking what looks like a crack pipe. It showed underage girls some say so China could black mail him. It also showed him in different sex acts with different women. Apparently, he liked looking at himself.

"Trump and his allies say there is evidence of corruption in emails and documents allegedly found on a laptop belonging to Democrat Joe Biden's son. They say those and other documents show that Hunter Biden used his father's influence to enrich himself through business deals in Ukraine and China, and that his father not only facilitated that, but may have benefited financially."[12]

Tony Bobulinski. A former business partner of Hunter Bidens came forward to give a press conference to clear his name of any wrong doing and Carlson Tucker also interviewed him. I seen the interview and it made me wonder, why isn't the DOJ or FBI talking to Bobulinski and trying to get to the bottom of these crimes? It is a mystery why nothing is being done about this lap top. Hunter, Joe, and Joe Biden's brother sold out Americans to China, Ukraine, Iran, and Russia. For some reason everyone wants to bury the story or deny it and it makes one wonder why? How far up does this go? Who else is involved?

When Joe Biden was asked about his son being on the board of Burisma he said he had no knowledge of what his son did. That is a bunch of bologna. What parent does not know what their child does for a living?

Two other witnesses have come forward; they turned over their cell phones, computers, and passwords. One is in jail and was moved after cooperating and the other is awaiting trial.

On 1-6-2021 all hell broke loose. They were counting and objecting to electoral votes and the certification of those votes. A massive amount of Trump supporters showed up in DC to support our President and stop the steal but that is not the way things went down. Mike Pence showed his true colors a traitor. He listened to the objections of all the voter fraud that took place but he did not even bother to overturn and votes. Then supporters as some say stormed the capital but some say it was Antifa dressed as Trump supporters so we really are not 100% sure. Antifa has been deemed as a terrorist group. Linked to the left and George Soros. They don't care about this country. They only care about the money and then they will move onto another place to torment. It has come down to patriots fighting our own government for all the corruption and all the fraud. Did the democrats and the spineless republicans that did not even have the back bone to defend us really think that the American people were going to take this? The American people for sure are tired of all the lies from the left and all the dirty scams and corruption. They are outraged at the fact this election was stolen from the people. We do not want to live under the Biden crime family. We don't want to be a communist country. We don't want to see the swamp get richer off the sweat of American backs. Big Tech plays a major role in all the corruption too. They have gotten too big for their britches and all of these elites think they are untouchable. They are going to get a big surprise when they find themselves in Gitmo or executed for treason. The irony here is there was a curfew in DC of 6 pm but they sure did not have that curfew when Antifa and BLM were terrorizing the city. I guess the rules change as they plot and scheme to see what scenario will benefit them.

On January 6, 2021 we have a new headline from CNN: US Capitol secured, 4 dead after rioters stormed the halls of Congress to block Biden's win By Ted Barrett, Manu Raju and Peter Nickeas, CNNUpdated 3:33 AM ET, Thu January 7, 2021 Of course the article goes on to say it was Trump supporters without any real evidence at the time and the fake news also followed suit. The hypocracy here is that a week later the news reported that a man named John Sullivan a BLM activist was arrested and heard saying the following "We got to get this s—t burned," and it's our house, he can be heard yelling at rioters, according to an affidavit signed by an FBI special agent." This was reported by the Washington Times. "I would also like to note that there are rumors going around that Antifa was involved dressed in MAGA apparel."[13] Will the American people ever know the truth? Why can't our main stream media just report facts? Why can't they investigate before spewing lies? At this point and time, we only have a few good news stations and I mean very few.

Don't forget what they did to General Flynn. They might call Trump supporters deplorable's but they are despicable.

I know these scandals were true but I felt like they constantly fed into them to keep us distracted on what was really on.

Chapter 7

President Donald Trumps' Accomplishments

"1. Almost 4 million jobs created since election
2. More Americans are now employed than ever recorded before in our history
3. Created more than 400,000 manufacturing jobs alone
4. The United States Has Brought the Leader of ISIS to Justice
5. Orders Additional Measures to Enhance Border Security
6. The United States Has Liberated All ISIS-Controlled Territory
7. Manufacturing jobs growing at the fastest rate in more than THREE DECADES
8. Unprecedented Support for Independent Living
9. Economic growth last quarter hit 4.2 percent
10. New unemployment claims recently hit a 49-year low
11. Median household income has hit highest level ever recorded
12. African-American unemployment has recently achieved the lowest rate ever recorded.
13. Hispanic-American unemployment is at the lowest rate ever recorded
14. Asian-American unemployment recently achieved the lowest rate ever recorded
15. End of Year Report: Deportations up 40% – Historically Low Crossings
16. Lowest unemployment rate ever recorded for Americans without a high school diploma.

17. Veterans' unemployment recently reached its lowest rate in nearly 20 years
18. ICE raid hits 77 businesses in Northern California
19. End of Year Report: Deportations up 40% – Historically Low Crossings
20. DHS: Announces New Procedures for Refugee Admissions
21. Deportations of Non criminals Rise as ICE Casts Wider Net
22. Almost 3.9 million Americans have been lifted off food stamps since the election
23. The Pledge to America's Workers has resulted in employers committing to train more than 4 million Americans
24. We are committed to VOCATIONAL education
25. 95 percent of U.S. manufacturers are optimistic about the future—the highest ever. Retail sales surged last month, up another 6 percent over last year
26. Signed the biggest package of tax cuts and reforms in history. After tax cuts, over $300 billion poured back in to the U.S. in the first quarter alone
27. As a result of our tax bill, small businesses will have the lowest top marginal tax rate in more than 80 years
28. Helped win U.S. bid for the 2028 Summer Olympics in Los Angeles
29. Helped win U.S.-Mexico-Canada's united bid for 2026 World Cup
30. Opened ANWR and approved Keystone XL and Dakota Access Pipelines
31. Trump has updated the travel ban to includes 8 more countries
32. Crossing the Border Illegally Is Harder Than It's Been In 50 Years
33. Withholding Federal Funds from Sanctuary Cities – Must allow ICE access to jails and notify before release
34. VA announces Access Standards for Health Care
35. Record number of regulations eliminated
36. Enacted regulatory relief for community banks and credit unions

37. Obamacare individual mandate penalty GONE
38. More affordable healthcare options for Americans through association health plans and short-term duration plans
39. The Trump Administration has constructed 100 miles of new border wall system
40. Currently, 167 miles of wall is under construction in high entry sectors such as San Diego, El Centro, El Paso, and Yuma
41. The new wall has contributed to a 56% overall decrease in the number of illegal migrant arrivals at the border
42. Under President Trump, the U.S. Border Patrol has arrested hundreds of members of dangerous gangs
43. Trump signs VA Mission Act
44. Enhancing Veteran Care Act
45. VA seeks partnerships to build and improve health-care facilities
46. VA announces Veterans Coordinated Access & Rewarding Experiences Act
47. VA, Ginnie Mae create task force to address mortgage refinancing issues
48. Telemedicine: An important tool for Veteran's health
49. Trump Signs Bill to Streamline VA Disability Claims Appeals Process
50. Ordered the killing of Qassem Soleimani, the head of Iran's elite Quds Force
51. President Trump fulfilled his promise to name Jerusalem Israel's capital city and moved the U.S. Embassy
52. Held two historic summits with North Korean leader Kim Jong Un, further demonstrating the Administration's commitment to a denuclearized Korean peninsula
53. President Trump withdrew the U.S. from the Iran Nuclear Agreement and instituted the toughest sanctions in history to drive the regime's oil exports to zero
54. Enacted regulatory relief for community banks and credit unions
55. Obamacare individual mandate penalty GONE

56. The Trump Administration is providing more affordable healthcare options for Americans through association health plans and short-term duration plans

57. The FDA approved more affordable generic drugs than ever before in history. Many drug companies are freezing or reversing planned price increases

58. Reformed the Medicare program to stop hospitals from overcharging low-income seniors on their drugs—saving seniors hundreds of millions of dollars this year alone

59. Signed Right-To-Try legislation

60. President Trump agreed to a phase one trade deal with China that includes a strong enforcement mechanism

61. President Trump withdrew the United States from the flawed Trans-Pacific Partnership

62. President Trump has forced our allies to recommit to NATO

63. Preventing Disability Discrimination in Ventilator Allocation Decisions During COVID-19

64. Secured $6 billion in NEW funding to fight the opioid epidemic

65. Have reduced high-dose opioid prescriptions by 16 percent during my first year in office

66. Signed VA Choice Act and VA Accountability Act, expanded VA telehealth services, walk-in-clinics, and same-day urgent primary and mental health care

67. Increased our coal exports by 60 percent; U.S. oil production recently reached all-time high

68. United States is a net natural gas exporter for the first time since 1957

69. Withdrew the United States from the job-killing Paris Climate Accord

70. Cancelled the illegal, anti-coal, so-called Clean Power Plan

71. Continues to reshape the Federal judiciary at a record pace

72. Has installed more federal court judges than any president in the past four decades

73. Following through on his promise to appoint judges who will uphold the
74. Constitution and rule of law for generations to come
75. President Trump has nominated, and the Senate has confirmed a grand total of 187 Article III judges
76. Secured record $700 billion in military funding
77. NATO allies are spending $69 billion more on defense since 2016
78. Process has begun to make the Space Force the 6th branch of the Armed Forces
79. Issued Executive Order to keep open Guantanamo Bay
80. Concluded a historic U.S.-Mexico Trade Deal to replace NAFTA
81. Protecting Rights and Preventing Abuse in Long-Term Care
82. Reached a breakthrough agreement with the E.U. to increase U.S. exports
83. Management of our nation's lands promotes conservation while encouraging good stewardship and expanding recreational opportunities
84. President Trump issued changes to the National Environmental Policy Act (NEPA) to reduce regulation and allow for infrastructure and transportation projects to move forward
85. Imposed tariffs on foreign steel and aluminum to protect our national security
86. Imposed tariffs on China in response to China's forced technology transfer, intellectual property theft, and their chronically abusive trade practices
87. Net exports are on track to increase by $59 billion this year
88. Trump signs 'Forever GI Bill,' boosting aid to student vets
89. VA expands Tele-Health access
90. VA fires more than 500 feds under Trump, even before new accountability law
91. Trump signs VA accountability act into law, promises better care for veterans

92. Trump Administration Streamlines Veteran Medical Records
93. Improved vetting and screening for refugees, and switched focus to overseas resettlement.
94. Protecting Against Disability Discrimination in State Triage Plan
95. The President rescinded President Obama's costly Clean Power Plan
96. The President proposed the Affordable Clean Energy Rule to reduce greenhouse gasses, empower states, promote energy independence, and facilitate economic growth and job creation
97. The Administration has rescinded many costly Obama-Era regulations including the methane emissions rule that would cost American energy developers an estimated $530 million annually Signed a sweeping new Farm Bill into law
98. Authorized the year-round sale of E15 gasoline which provided a boost to America's corn growing communities
99. Red tape that has harmed American farmers have been rolled back
100. Christian refugees admitted now outnumber Muslim refugees admitted."

All Information was obtained from the we love trump website. The link is https://welovetrump.com/2020/08/17/how-much-do-you-know-a-101-list-of-president-trumps-accomplishments/ written by shya

I encourage all readers to go to this website and read their other articles.

Chapter 8

Joe Biden's Accomplishment In 47 Years

"1973 Biden enters politics ...

1977 *Biden fights to keep schools segregated because in his own words, "allowing blacks to integrate would create a racial jungle" Fact check me.

1983 *BIDEN Taxes Social Security*

1988 *Ran for president but had to end his campaign after getting busted for plagiarism.

1993 *BIDEN Taxes Social Security, AGAIN*

1994 ***Biden writes the "Stop and Frisk" law which is what blacks blame for "systemic racism" today. This law took millions of black men from their homes and transplanted them into prison. Way to go Joe. This was Biden's biggest accomplishment in 47 years of elected office. Factcheck me, it's true.

2008 Calls Obama the first "articulate" and "clean" mainstream African-American.

2020: NOW HE'S READY TO FIX THE COUNTRY."[1]

https://welovetrump.com/2021/04/04/fair-is-fair-47-years-of-joe-bidens-accomplishments/

Information taken from the we love Trump site. I encourage all readers to take a look at the site. The article was written by Noah. As the fake President he has managed to make some disastrous decisions, not made by thinking of the American People but rather out of revenge. He is trying to undo all that President Trump had accomplished.

We have a crisis at the border, gas prices are rising, he is not standing behind Israel, he shut down the key stone pipe line and people are out of work. Inflation is rising. This country is in a mess.

He lied about marching in the civil right movement. I don't know why he did that. I was watching a video of Charlamagne tha God where Biden insulted the host by saying something to the effect that if you don't know if you are for me or Trump then you ain't black. Who does that?

Biden is not forth coming about his son Hunter Biden and his work in Ukraine. He claims he does not know what his son's business ventures are, but that is not true and has been proven in emails that surfaced, besides that what parent does not know what their child does for a living.

Chapter 9

President Trump

Donald President Trump was not a politician he was a business man. Maybe that is what the American people needed. They need someone different to get into office and shake things up. Donald Trump was the man for the job. He was not a follower; he could not be bullied and he could not be bought.

He ran his first campaign on make America great again (MAGA) and drain the swamp and believe me we had plenty of dirty politicians in our government. Those slimy creatures were slithering all over Washington D.C. They were getting rich off the American people and lining their own pockets. We were basically their slaves. They were living high on the hog while the average American was struggling. We only had a few good politicians but they could not take on D.C. alone, it would have been political suicide. Donald Trump is the only president that I know of, that worked for free and worked for the people. He had a good life before he started campaigning. Why would a man that had everything throw it away for others? I will tell you what I think. He did it because he saw how bad and corrupt our government had become.

I must admit in the beginning I was so worried that someone would try to assassinate him but he came out unscathed. I think most democrats hated him and some of them did everything they could to get him out of office but our president was always one step ahead of them. They were so disrespectful to him and they did not even try to hide their contempt. They were constantly accusing him of things he did not do but I noticed that whenever they accused him of something it was something that they were really doing. We all began to see a pattern with the slithering swamp creatures and you were always wondering what they would do next. Don't worry the swamp creatures never let you down; they always had something else up their sleeve. It was always something vile. I don't know how the man ever got anything done fighting off the mob of swamp creatures. He really did work day and night and often long hours. He was resilient. He had more energy than people half his age. People that worked with him had a hard time keeping up with him.

The president could not even make a joke without the media or democrats making something horrible out it. In other words, they put their own spin on his words and twist them to fit their own agenda. They were so full of hate that they sure did not set a good example for Americans and our youth. He exposed them by letting them carry on with their wicked ways and really, they ended up exposing themselves.

Some people did not like the Presidents tweets oh well he is only human and he has got to get the message out there some way since we are being censored by the media, big tech, and social media. Some people did not even vote for him because of his tweets. Instead of looking at what he did for our country they were worried about his tweets. I have seen AOC put out some hateful tweets.

Our President started what they called operation warp speed and the objective was to get a vaccine out quickly without all the red tape. Something is a little fishy. On November 9, 2020 it was reported by CNN that Pfizer had a vaccine that was 90% effective and was awaiting FDA approval but then on November 16, 2020 CBS reported that Moderna had a vaccine that was 94.5% effective. Pfizer comes out again on CNBC, November 18, 2020 and now says their vaccine is 95% effective. This is enough to make a person worry. President Trump is the first on in history that has ever been able to accomplish something of this nature so quickly.

They majority of the people loved Trump and they would even

say so at his rallies. His rallies drew the biggest crowds that we have ever seen for a President and they were so full of energy. Even when the election was up in the air, he still held rallies and you still seen then massive crowds, the love, and the support. I remember one rally where he seen three young men dancing and he invited them up on the stage to dance.

President did good things before he was even president of the United States. "As Martin Luther King Jr.'s niece, **Alveda King said: "Trump is not a racist"**.[1]

Trump has never based his loyalty around skin color, there are those who will argue the only color Trump see's is the color of money, but the truth is, he's earned his bounty and shared it just the same by blessing communities, foundations, schools, minority groups, institutions, the arts programs, sports, children's groups, the under-privileged, and others, especially, NYC.

Let us not forget the tragedy of 9/11, when citizen Trump spent his own time, money, and manpower to support and help restore New York City, his home, and the people he loved unconditionally.[2]

"Did you know that civilian Donald Trump had a two-year personal relationship with the black model, Kara Young in 1998, she herself stated, I never heard him say a disparaging comment towards any race of people. Is this the character of a white supremacist-racist?"[3]

Joe Biden has made many racial comments but your main stream media will not talk about that.

1. As recently as June of 2019, Biden praised the "civility" of the segregationist senators he worked with in Congress to pass anti-busing legislation.
2. Biden praised the notorious segregationist politician George Wallace, boasted about how Wallace once honored him with an award in 1973, and told a Southern audience in 1987 that "we [Delawareans] were on the South's side in the Civil War."
3. Biden opposed busing in the 1970s and expressed fears that it would lead to a "racial jungle."

4. Biden voted to protect the tax-exempt status of private segregated schools.
5. Biden told black radio host Charlamagne tha God, "If you have a problem figuring out whether you're for me or Trump, then you ain't black."
6. Biden told the Asian and Latino Coalition of Des Moines that "poor kids are just as bright and just as talented as white kids."
7. While delivering remarks before a black audience in Delaware, Biden launched into a meandering story about a gang leader named Corn Pop and claimed that he "learned about roaches" while working at a community pool in a black neighborhood.
8. In 2008, Biden referred to then presidential candidate Barack Obama as "the first sort of mainstream African-American who is articulate and bright and clean."
9. In 2006, Biden told C-SPAN, "You cannot go to a 7-Eleven or a Dunkin' Donuts unless you have a slight Indian accent."
10. Biden falsely claimed to have "marched" in the civil rights movement.[4] If President Trump would have done or said any of these things, they would have crucified him in the media.

Some have called our President a white supremacist and that is not true. They have even asked him to denounce white supremacy which he has over and over again but the hypocrisy here is that they will not ask Joe Biden to denounce BLM or Antifa.

That old saying you can't judge a book by its cover is true in the case of President Trump.

Chapter 10

The Presidential Election

What happened to the Presidential Election? My husband and I watched the Presidential Election on the television and when we went to bed at 10 pm President Trump was ahead but when we got up the next morning, all of the sudden Joe Biden was ahead. We knew something was not right because usually you know the night of or the next day who the President is but that was not the case. It is now December 10th of 2020 and we still do not know who the President is.

As the day progressed it looks like Joe Biden was still in the lead and that is just impossible. This is the man that refused to answer questions on court packing and the scandal surrounding his family with Hunter Biden's lap top. I smell swamp creatures slithering around this election. This is the same man that did not even have the crowds at his rallies the way Trump did. Bid might have had a hand full of people but Trump had thousands.

Wow, Sidney Powell dropped a bombshell. Powell was on Newmax with Howie Carr. She confirmed that Eric Coomer of Dominion was on a call with Antifa. She also said Dominion has moved their offices and Coomer has disappeared. He is probably on the run if he is not dead.

The scandals and corruption are like the energizer bunny they keep going and going. "Last week, CDP posted a story about how democrats were conspiring with rouge agents in the <u>Central Intelligence Agency</u> in order to utilize a tool called <u>SCORECARD</u>"[1].

"Sidney Powell says her next venture is to explain these statistical anomalies to the public, showing how it is mathematically impossible for the election as it is currently being reported by the corporate media to be honest and fair."[2]

The voter fraud suits continue. It is the day after Thanksgiving and law suits are still going on over the voter fraud. Sidney Powell filed lawsuits in Georgia and Michigan late Wednesday, continuing efforts to reveal alleged voter fraud that she claims rigged President Trump of an election triumph.

Both cases revolve around issues related to voting machines, mail-in ballots, and the late Venezuelan dictator Hugo Chavez, <u>according to *Bloomberg*</u>.[3]

"Former Kansas Attorney General Phil Kline said Wednesday that Facebook CEO Mark Zuckerberg gave a large sum of money to nonprofit groups that ultimately used the cash to dictate how states run their elections."[4] To me I see this as Zuckerberg trying to influence the election. Why is he doing this? What is his agenda? Zuckerberg needs to stick with his computers and leave elections alone. I guess he forgot about the little people that helped make him rich.

Some of us already know that there is an audit going on in Maricopa County in Arizona but for some reason democrats have been trying to shut it down. Why? What are they hiding? They make themselves look guilty by their actions. From what I understand other states are prepared to follow suit in having an audit done. The innocent want to make sure that something like this never happens again to anyone running for office.

It will be interesting to see what the come of the audits will be in all the states that are going to participate. This election in my opinion was stolen from us. I also believe that everyone should present an ID when voting. My state of Indiana made us show ID. We show ID for just about anything else. We show a picture ID when picking up prescriptions, going to the doctors, buying liquor and even in some places buying cigarettes.

I knew from the beginning when they started this whole mail in ballot idea that there was going to be some cheating and some people have already been prosecuted for voter fraud.

Chapter 11

Behind The Scenes

It is like watching a bad movie; on January 7th, 2021 they started putting a fence with barb wire around the Capital. Two weeks before the fake Joe Biden's fake inauguration, The National Guard was sent to the Capital to help with the fake inauguration.

Yes, I said fake Joe Biden. There is no way that I will believe that the man claiming to be Joe Biden is the real Joe Biden. The Joe Biden I remember had blue eyes this guy has either dark brown or black eyes. Something is not right. I also said fake inauguration because we all know that there was voter fraud. This election was stolen from the people.

The fake inauguration was a joke from the small clips I seen on television. Biden still did not have as many people at his rallies as President Trump did for his rallies.

On his first day they showed him signing some executive orders to undo all the orders that President Trump put into effect. The Democrats and Biden have so much hatred for Trump that they can't see straight. They don't care if Trump's policies were good or not, they just want to undo everything he did out of spite.

It really makes you wonder if this whole corona virus thing was blown out of proportion to keep us distracted from something else that is going on. I believe that the virus is real but I don't think it is worse than N1H1. I don't think we all need to quarantine or wear mask.

Then you have the media calling the QAnon group a conspiracy theory. We have always had conspiracies. When does a conspiracy stop being a conspiracy? We even had conspiracy television shows. It makes one wonder why they protest the QAnon group. Could it be that they are afraid that this group is getting too close to what is going on and that maybe there is some truth in what they are saying? If you do not have anything to hide then why worry about what some group says. Do you remember when the government and media claimed that UFOs were a conspiracy theory and now, they say they are real? They have been looking for the lockness monster and big foot since I was a child as well. They claim to have caught images on camera but no one has ever captured a live one that I know of. It does not mean that these beings do not exist.

The funniest thing is that the Democrats are trying to impeach Trump again. He is not even in the White House and according to the Media and Democrats Biden is our new President. Trump had a rally on January 6, 2021 and he was not even done with his speech when the capital was invaded. Furthermore, he did not even say one word or ask anyone to do anything criminal. This movie just has a lot of twist and turns.

Sometimes it is hard to tell the good guys from the bad guys but we do have some great characters in this movie for example we have Diamond and Silk these two women are up lifting. They tell the truth whether you like it or not with a little humor. Then you have the lovely Candace Owens. You cannot bully or intimidate this woman and she is also a straight shooter. We have Kayleigh McEnany who was President Trump's press secretary and she was always organized and prepared for her press briefing and she could put those rude reporters and journalist in their place. Also, we have Terrence Williams, he truly loves President Trump and he will defend him but Terrence has paid the price for it. Social media has censored him, trying to shut him up, and then they tried banning his book. You still can't stop Terrence. We have Dan Bongino that was a police officer and in the Secret Service and he is a straight and honest shooter. God Bless Him.

Every bad movie has a villain so we will pick Nancy Pelosi to play the villain and her puppet Chuck Schumer and their little radical cronies. These people are ruthless and the only things they care about are power and money.

Chapter 12

They Are All Connected

I have found in my research that all the big players in the Covid 19 pandemic that terrified most Americans along with the main stream media are connected. Fauci has had an ongoing relationship with Gates. Gates is not a doctor or scientist that I know of. I do not know what they have common.

"On April 1, the emails show, Fauci spoke by phone with Gates about a global vaccine effort. The doctor said he was "enthusiastic about moving forward on a collaborative and hopefully synergistic approach to COVID-19" involving federal health agencies and the Bill and Melinda Gates Foundation, according to the emails."[1]

Now I get the big picture these two want to work together on vaccinations. I am terrified now.

"Judicial Watch announced that it and the Daily Caller News Foundation received 301 pages of emails of Dr. Anthony Fauci from the U.S. Department of Health and Human Services showing that National Institutes of Health (NIH) officials tailored confidentiality forms to China's terms and that the World Health Organization (WHO) conducted an unreleased, "strictly confidential" Covid-19 epidemiological analysis in January 2020."[2] Here is the connection between Fauci, the NIH and the WHO. I believe this is why President Trump pulled out of the WHO and rightfully so.

Here is a little back ground on Dr. Fauci, he started his career with the National Institute of Allergy and Infectious Diseases (NIAID).

In 1984 he became the director of the NIAID (3) Most of you might remember him as working on the AIDS virus. Dr. Christine Grady is married to Dr. Fauci. Dr. Christine Grady is currently chief of the Department of Bioethics at the National Institutes of Health (NIH). I feel this is a conflict of interest that all these organizations were involved with China. Then you have Gates partners with Fauci. Joanne Grady (Christines sister) is married to James Huskey whom worked for foreign affairs. This is kind of awkward. I can't connect the dots between Bill Gates and James Huskey.

I do know that Bill Gates and Dr. Fauci both had ties to Moderna. Now we get to some more connections.

Here is the scary part. "Dr. Fauci personally licensed and saw to the performance of clinical trials to create a vaccine for the H5N1 pandemic that was previously declared by Fauci. The company that Fauci worked with to create and stockpile a vaccine for the avian flu was Sanofi Pasteur:

The FDA has licensed Sanofi Pasteur's H5N1 vaccine, the first avian flu vaccine for humans. Sanofi Pasteur, in collaboration with the National Institutes of Health, submitted a BLA to the FDA for the vaccine." "Sanofi Pasteur is related to one of the very first western labs located in the Republic of China. One of its investors is George Soros.

"George Soros also invests in a company in Wuhan, China, where the Coronavirus outbreak began. That company is called Wuxi AppTech, which just so happens, they develop vaccines too. This company is also related to the former Head of the China Communist Party, Jiang Zemin."[3] I am sure by now you can see the links between the big players. One must ask what, were all these players up to? What was their agenda? I have my own opinion but I want you to draw your own conclusions. Why were they all working for China or the Wuhan lab?

"The National Institutes of Health earmarked $600,000 for the Wuhan Institute of Virology over a five-year period to study whether bat coronaviruses could be transmitted to humans, White House chief medical adviser Dr. Anthony Fauci told lawmakers Tuesday."

"Fauci, the head of the National Institute of Allergy and Infectious

Diseases (NIAID), told a House Appropriations subcommittee that the money was funneled to the Chinese lab through the non-profit EcoHealth Alliance to fund a modest collaboration with very respectable Chinese scientists who were world experts on coronavirus."

But "Fauci emphatically denied that the money went toward so-called gain of function research, which he described as taking a virus that could infect humans and making it either more transmissible and/or pathogenic for humans."[4] Why was the US sending them money? The NIH under Fauci should be held accountable.

"I watched Senator John Kennedy question Dr. Fauci and I had to laugh when Senator John Kennedy asked Fauci:

(Kennedy: "Here's where I'm getting at: You gave them money, and you said, 'Don't do gain-of-function research.

Fauci: "Correct."

Kennedy: "And they said, 'We won't.'"

Fauci: "Correct."

Kennedy: "And you have no way of knowing whether they did or not, except you trust them. Is that right?

auci: "Well, **we generally always trust the grantee to do what they say**, and you look at the results—

Kennedy: **"Have you ever had a grantee lie to you?**

Fauci: **"I cannot guarantee that a grantee has not lied to us because you never know."**[5]

I don't know about the rest of you but we should have never sent any money to China for experiments or research. The only way any experiments or research should have been done is here in the United States.

For those of you that do not know the meaning of gain of function. It is taking a virus and manipulating it to be more infectious or deadly. What are your thoughts on gain of function? The thought I have is that no good can come from such an experiment.

I know that Dr. Fauci has been questioned by several Senators and Senator Rand Paul does not let Fauci get away with anything.

Now we get to Kamala Harris who was once a district attorney. She set up a fund to help release some violent criminals. I thought this woman took an oath to serve and protect.

This was on her twitter page. She must be tied to these criminals in some way or another. "A FOX 9 report from August revealed that the organization bailed out individuals including Darnika Floyd, who was charged with second-degree murder after allegedly stabbing a friend to death, and Christopher Boswell, who is facing charges of sexual assault and kidnapping. The group put up $100,000 on behalf of Floyd and $350,000 on behalf of Boswell."⁶ If you read about her years as an attorney she was not much to brag about in fact she could make one sick. She was a disgrace to the profession. "Beginning in 2012 George Soro's led a four-year, $16 million campaign to change California Criminal Policy, which Kamala Harris was deeply involved with as California Attorney General." (10) Now we have the Harris and Soro's connection. I hope everyone can also see the hyprocacy here as well. A woman about to be VP of the United States shielding criminals is unacceptable. Just think of the families that suffer because of her lack of judgement.

Chapter 13

Final Thoughts

I learned in 2020 that you cannot trust our main stream media or most organizations that have three letters, for example the FBI, DOJ, CIA, CDC, NIH the WHO and many others.

I have learned that you need to dig deep to find the truth. Ask the questions who, what, when, where, why and how. Find out who the key players are.

Do not be afraid to research what bills are before the house, senate, or congress. Watch some of the judiciary videos and videos of congress.

Don't accept an answer just because an expert said so or the government said so. That is how we got into the whole lock down and mask mandate to begin with.

Some of my favorite people to watch are Candace Owens, Diamond and Silk, Senator Ted Cruz, Rand Paul, Devin Nunez, and Terrence Williams they tried to ban his book just because he is a Trump supporter. I love Dan Bongino. He was in the secret service so I find him very credible. I also love watching Marsha Blackburn.

Don't let big tech censor you. Find other alternatives to be heard.

We need to take our country back from those that have been ripping us off for years.

All of the money that the government has spent on the Wuhan lab and other crazy things that we did not sign up for could be going to help the medical cost in this country. We need to take of our own first before helping other countries. We need to take care or our vets and homeless. No one should be homeless in the United States.

Our Soldiers have given their all and some even their lives to protect our rights and it angers me that they are not shown the respect they deserve by some. It is true they fought for our right to free speech even for those that use it just to be nasty. I am talking about this cancel culture. Mr. Potato Head never did anything to anybody but yet they want to exclude the word Mr. Why? As a kid we did not care that it was called Mr. Potato head. Someone just got the bright idea that it was offensive and they were going to change the name just because they could. I had a problem with them requesting nativity sets be taken down one year. It is our right to have them on our property and if they don't like it, then don't go past my home.

We can no longer stand by and be silent. We must hold China accountable for unleashing this deadly virus on the world. We have given too much power to big tech and now thru their censorship they decide what we need to hear and what we don't need to hear. It is time for us to take our power and rights back. They are attacking our rights to free speech just because it offends them or does not fit there narrative. They need to be held accountable because they censored many other doctors and scientist that could have helped saved lives. The same goes for twitter and google and YouTube.

We need to do something about big pharma and getting medical cost down and prescription drug prices. Some people die needlessly because they can't afford to go to the doctors or hospital.

We need to hold the media accountable for not reporting on important issues or keeping information from us on alternative treatments and alternative medicines. They need to be held accountable for suppressing the Hunter Biden laptop scandal and other scandals that did not fit their narrative.

We need to hold any and all politicians accountable that were voted to represent "we the people" but got too big for their britches and went rogue on us.

This country needs to repent and we need God more than ever. It might be time for us to take a step back instead of always advancing because it appears that with advancement comes corruption.

I remember when I was a child we could not wait to get outside and play and I think we were in better physical shape. These children today just want to be on the internet and play video games all day. I call these electronic baby sitters. Technology in some ways is ruining our lives. I see kids and adults looking at their cell phones constantly. Remember the days when we did not have cell phones. We lived just fine. I have a cell phone but I barely use it and I don't really want too. I would rather you pick up the phone and call me than to text me.

All of these things are just distractions so you do not know what is really going on in our government.

Slowly we lost sight of the importance of God and family. There is one thing good that came out of this pandemic and that was I got closer to God.

I believe that things will get worse before they get better. Just stay vigilante and positive. If you see something that looks suspicious call the police, it is better to be safe than sorry.

Citings

Introduction

1. https://abcnews.go.com/Health/timeline-coronavirus-started/story?id=69435165
2. https://abc7ny.com/first-coronavirus-case-us-of-covid-america-patient-one-dr-george-diaz/9871792/
3. https://www.foxnews.com/world/chinese-virologist-coronavirus-cover-up-flee-hong-kong-whistleblower
4. https://abcnews.go.com/Health/timeline-coronavirus-started/story?id=69435165
5. https://www.forbes.com/sites/geoffwhitmore/2020/10/19/when-did-president-trump-ban-travel-from-china-and-can-you-travel-to-china-now/?sh=5ef9638d7484

Chapter 1

1. https://www.theatlantic.com/politics/archive/2020/04/world-health-organization-blame-pandemic-coronavirus/609820/
2. https://www.foxnews.com/world/who-was-li-wenliang-the-chinese-doctor-who-warned-about-the-coronavirus
3. https://www.youtube.com/watch?v=PKMJiiCyhVc
4. https://video.foxnews.com/v/6198164324001#sp=show-clips
5. https://nypost.com/2020/04/29/dr-fauci-backed-controversial-wuhan-lab-studying-coronavirus/
6. https://youtu.be/CmllqkU6j2k
7. https://www.nationalreview.com/corner/yes-biden-called-trumps-travel-restrictions-xenophobic/
8. https://www.foxnews.com/politics/flashback-obama-admin-halted-state-h1n1-testing-complicating-bidens-attacks-on-white-house

9   https://www.msn.com/en-us/news/politics/dianne-feinstein-is-pictured-walking-through-dc-airport-without-a-mask/ar-BB19wkbh

10 https://www.bing.com/videos/search?q=fauci+on+youtube+at+game+not+wearing+a+mask&docid=608030918109253511&mid=DB564EB332195306A179DB564EB332195306A179&view=detail&FORM=VIRE

11 https://www.dailymail.co.uk/news/article-8866415/Chris-Cuomo-threatened-fine-apartment-building-seen-without-mask.html

12 https://www.washingtonexaminer.com/news/five-governors-cuomo-covid-19-positive-patients-nursing-homes

13 https://www.cnbc.com/2020/07/29/dr-fauci-says-all-the-valid-scientific-data-shows-hydroxychloroquine-isnt-effective-in-treating-coronavirus.html

14 https://www.youtube.com/watch?v=0oSGIC_irVs

15 https://www.youtube.com/watch?v=2uzXHnUViro

16 https://www.silverdoctors.com/headlines/world-news/factory-that-manufactures-hydroxychloroquine-mysteriously-bursts-into-flames-explodes/

17 CDC Study Finds Overwhelming Majority Of People Getting Coronavirus Wore Masks

Chapter 2

1   https://nationalinterest.org/blog/reboot/scotus-constitution-still-applies-even-during-pandemic-173909

2   https://www.investopedia.com/coronavirus-aid-relief-and-economic-security-cares-act-4800707

3   https://dailycaller.com/2020/05/12/pelosi-coronavirus-bill-25-billion-post-office-bailout/

4   https://www.cnbc.com/2020/10/15/mnuchin-says-hell-give-ground-on-virus-testing-in-stimulus-negotiations-with-pelosi.html

5   https://www.westernjournal.com/trey-gowdy-madder-pelosi-true-covid-relief-strategy-slip/

6   **https://channel411news.com/2020/11/20/mnuchin-says-he-and-gop-leaders-will-discuss-plan-to-pass-targeted-stimulus-with-democrats-help/**

7   https://redstate.com/bonchie/2020/10/27/californias-new-thanksgiving-covid-restrictions-are-a-dystopian-nightmare-n270376

8   https://duckduckgo.com/?t=ffab&q=California+Gov.+Gavin+Newsom+(D)+has+found+himself+in+the+same+hot+water+that+House+Speaker+Nancy+Pelosi+(D-Calif.)+was+in+after+her+hair+salon+trip+this+summer%2C+in+his+case+for+a+dinner+at+Napa+County%E2%80%99s+ultra-exclusive+French+Laundry+&ia=web

Chapter 3

1   https://duckduckgo.com/?t=ffab&q=+++Dr.+Fauci%2C+"is+an+American+ physicia+and+immunologist+who+has+served

2   https://duckduckgo.com/?t=ffab&q=%E2%80%9C+Anthony+Fauci+ Plotted+%E2%80%98Global+Vaccine+Action+Plan%E2%80%99 +with+Bill+Gates+Before+Pushing+COVID+Panic+and+Doubts+About+ Hydroxychloroquine+Treatments.%E2%80%9D+(2)&ia=web

3   https://www.nationalgeographic.com/science/article/anthony-fauci-no-scientific-evidence-the-coronavirus-was-made-in-a-chinese-lab-cvd

4   https://www.worldtribune.com/emails-show-fauci-nih-who-accommodated-china-on-covid-confidentiality-terms/

5   https://www.medicinenet.com/script/main/art.asp?articlekey=230460

6   https://www.foxnews.com/media/physician-blasts-cdc-coronavirus-death-count-guidelines

7   https://www.foxnews.com/media/physician-blasts-cdc-coronavirus-death-count-guidelines

8   https://principia-scientific.com/nih-stanford-study-proves-face-masks-worthless-against-covid/

9   https://www.news.com.au/technology/science/mit-researchers-say-sixfoot-rule-behind-social-distancing-policies-has-no-physical-basis/news-story/ f6e782b07e736fc7042e541317a4c346

10   https://principia-scientific.com/so-far-27-studies-prove-lockdowns-have-little-to-no-effect/

Chapter 4

1   https://www.nbcnews.com/news/us-news/portland-protesters-tear-down-statues-abraham-lincoln-theodore-roosevelt-n1242913

2   https://abcnews.go.com/US/portland-police-declare-riot-100th-straight-night-protests/story?id=72846185

3   https://www.nbcwashington.com/news/local/virginia-state-senator-charged-with-injury-to-confederate-monument/2393228/

4   https://www.judicialwatch.org/press-releases/judge-orders-antifa-activist-yvette-felarca-to-pay-judicial-watch-legal-fees-for-her-entirely-frivolous-lawsuit/

5   https://www.youtube.com/watch?v=QpPS9IWXSa4

6   https://www.chicagotribune.com/columns/rex-huppke/ct-paid-protesters-huppke-20170227-story.html

7   https://www.youtube.com/watch?v=op1yqcIdhbE

8   https://www.cnn.com/2020/06/03/us/david-dorn-st-louis-police-shot-trnd/
     index.html

9   https://www.foxbusiness.com/politics/black-lives-matter-has-been-
     hijacked-by-george-soros-sheriff-clarke

10 https://nypost.com/2020/06/25/blm-co-founder-describes-herself-as-
     trained-marxist/

11 https://www.the-sun.com/news/2998524/blm-founder-quit-ugly-truth/

Chapter 5

1   https://www.breitbart.com/the-media/2013/06/13/washington-post-family-
     relations-between-media-obama-officials-does-not-affect-coverage/

2   https://ipatriot.com/liberal-democrats-incestuous-media-relationships/

3   https://www.youtube.com/watch?v=hAZphlEzPNc.

4   https://www.washingtontimes.com/news/2020/nov/6/candace-owens-
     sues-facebook-fact-checkers-defamati/

5   https://www.foxnews.com/politics/candace-owens-targets-facebook-3rd-
     party-fact-checkers-with-lawsuit

6   https://www.thegatewaypundit.com/2020/09/former-fox-news-host-bill-
     oreilly-defends-newt-gingrich-network-flap-george-soros-video/

7   https://thepatriotgazette.com/soros-backed-la-d-a-george-gascon-
     reportedly-cutting-the-countys-hardcore-gang-unit-and-narcotics-units-
     in-half/

8   https://thepatriotgazette.com/soros-backed-la-d-a-george-gascon-
     reportedly-cutting-the-countys-hardcore-gang-unit-and-narcotics-units-
     in-half/

9   https://www.thegatewaypundit.com/2019/12/huge-ag-bill-barr-calls-out-
     george-soros-for-subverting-legal-system-and-causing-more-chaos-and-
     more-victims-through-support-of-radical-candidates/

Chapter 6

1   https://www.judiciary.senate.gov/press/rep/releases/judiciary-committee-
     releases-transcripts-of-interviews-conducted-during-oversight-of-crossfire-
     hurricane-investigation

2   https://www.cnn.com/2020/03/11/us/harvey-weinstein-sentence/index.html

3   https://www.thebalance.com/fundamentals-of-the-2020-market-
     crash-4799950

4   https://blacklivesmatter.com/herstory/https://en.wikipedia.org/wiki/Antifa
     (United States)

5   https://en.wikipedia.org/wiki/Antifa (United States)

6   https://nypost.com/2020/10/04/nyc-woman-says-ghislaine-maxwell-gagged-and-raped-her/

7   https://www.cnbc.com/2020/07/29/ghislaine-maxwell-accused-jeffrey-epstein-accomplice-claims-violation.html

8   https://www.cnn.com/2020/08/04/middleeast/beirut-explosion-port-intl/index.html

9   https://www.nbcnews.com/politics/2020-election/biden-slams-trump-climate-arsonist-fires-ravage-west-n1240063

10   https://www.history.com/topics/womens-rights/roe-v-wade

11   https://nypost.com/2020/10/31/feds-reportedly-seized-second-hunter-biden-laptop-in-fe

12   https://www.nbcnews.com/politics/2020-election/here-s-what-happened-when-nbc-news

13   https://www.cbs58.com/news/capitol-is-on-lockdown-as-pro-trump-demonstrators-try-to

Chapter 7

1   https://frankreport.com/2020/04/18/one-hundred-twenty-five-amazing-accomplishments-of-president-donald-j-trump/

Chapter 8

1   https://www.miamidadedems.org/joe-biden-accomplishments-list

2   https://thehill.com/opinion/campaign/499065-lies-damned-lies-and-the-truth-about-joe-biden

3   https://americanmilitarynews.com/2019/06/obamas-ice-chief-illegal-immigrant-cages-were-built-by-the-obama-administration/

Chapter 9

1   https://thehill.com/blogs/blog-briefing-room/news/456749-martin-luther-king-jrs-niece-trump-is-not-a-racist

2   https://americaoutloud.com/who-was-donald-j-trump-before-he-became-president-of-the-united-states/

3   https://duckduckgo.com/?t=ffab&q=Donald+Trump+had+a+two-year+personal+relationship+with+the+black+model%2C+Kara+Young+in+1998%2C&ia=web

4   https://www.breitbart.com/politics/2019/06/03/joe-biden-lied-in-1987-with-claim-he-marched-in-civil-rights-movement/

Chapter 10

1 https://conservativedailypost.com/evidence-cia-scorecard-and-the-hammer-used-to-alter-election-counting-machines-for-biden/

2 https://duckduckgo.com/?t=ffab&q=Powell+says+her+next+venture+is+to+explain+these+statistical+anomalies+to+the+public&ia=web

3 https://duckduckgo.com/?t=ffab&q=Both+cases+revolve+around+issues+related+to+voting+machines%2C+mail-in+ballots%2C+and+the+late+Venezuelan+dictator+Hugo+Chavez%2C+according+to+Bloomberg.&ia=web

4 https://politicalvelcraft.org/2020/12/26/mark-zuckerberg-out-spent-u-s-government-financing-the-u-s-elections/

Chapter 11

Chapter 12

1 https://welovetrump.com/2021/06/02/new-emails-highlight-the-gates-and-fauci-connection/

2 https://www.judicialwatch.org/press-releases/emails-who-terms/

3 https://genzconservative.com/fauci-china-connection/

4 https://nypost.com/2021/05/25/fauci-admits-nih-funding-of-wuhan-lab-denies-gain-of-functio

5 https://www.msn.com/en-us/news/politics/sen-kennedy-confronts-fauci-on-funding-of-chinese-labs-how-do-you-know-they-didn-t-lie-to-you/ar-AAKpHx5

6 https://www.foxnews.com/politics/bail-fund-kamala-harris-thomas-moseley

Printed in the United States
by Baker & Taylor Publisher Services